I dedicate this book to the memory of Constantinos Cavafis, unworthy of him as it is, and to my two children, Robin and Sophie. May their journey to Ithaca be a long one.

CONTENTS

INTRODUCTION

The poetry of Constantinos Cavafis (also known as Cavafy) has been my spiritual food for many years now. He was a part of my discovery of the 'miracle period' in modern Greek culture, a time when no other country had as many brilliant poets or popular composers, or such creative energy. For me it began when a waiter in Corfu about thirty years ago told me that the marvellous music I was hearing in all the tavernas was not traditional at all, as I had assumed, but was created by serious composers who were building on the demotic heritage. This was a time when Greek waiters loved to spend time talking about Greek politics and culture with interested foreigners, and I became familiar with names such as Xarhakos, Hadjidakis and Theodorakis. If I was in Athens (and not knowing where else to look) I scoured Monastiraki market for the tape cassettes. I grew to love the passionate and rich singing of such as Maria Fandouri and Nena Venetsanou.

The composers were setting to music the poetry of writers such as Yiannis Ritsos and Nikos Gatsos. It was a time when the best composers in the world were combining with the best lyricists to produce the best and most intelligent popular music. Naturally, I became interested in the poets that everyone kept mentioning, but I soon became aware that many people had a special reverence for someone called Cavafy, whose work was a precursor to the miracle period. Some of his poetry has been set to music, and Leonard Cohen obviously borrowed liberally from 'The God Forsakes Antony' to write his stunningly beautiful 'Alexandra Leaving'.

Like most foreigners I came to Cavafy through his two most famous poems, 'Ithaca' and 'Waiting for the Barbarians', which I found in Kimon Friar's *Modern Greek Poetry* (1982), but it wasn't long before I had all the translations I could find. All of them have something to recommend them, although I do have my favourites.

Cavafy (1863–1933), an Alexandrian Greek, led a relatively humble and obscure life, writing poems mainly for a small circle of friends. It seems he was a perfectionist and kept only a tiny proportion of what he wrote. His two great obsessions were beautiful young men and the Panhellenic ancient world. I must admit I get tired of reading about the former, who are always up to their necks in 'sensual delights', but these poems have the enormous merit of being absolutely honest in their eroticism, their nostalgia, their guiltlessness and their pain, without ever being explicit or vulgar. That is a good way to celebrate sex and love, regardless of one's orientation. In addition to these two types of poems there are a number that you might describe as 'philosophical', and, of course, the categories do get mixed up.

Cavafy is a poet who never leaves you. He gets under your skin. He creates cameos of characters that you remember

IMAGINING ALEXANDRIA

OTHER LIVES

In one life there was a man
Naked and brown, ripped by briars,
Trapping conies on the South Downs
For the woman and the child;
Exchanging furs for salt and fish
On the pebble beach;
Gathering driftwood for winter fires,
While the woman rooted for tubers,
The child learned snaring,
And sages read the runes of time
In the strange movement of the wanderers.

In another life there was a woman,
Dead in childbed with her fifth child,
Leaving a man to scratch a life,
Ploughing on the brown horizon;
Hoping for another woman,
For his daughters to be grown;
And the priest talked of God's will,
Of Good Grace and Providence.

In another life there was a man
Grown sleek on inequalities, but
Always servant of the same desires
Up for market in the wide world;

While the woman wove,
Her heart bound fast,
Her passions unconceived,
Her body like the Downs,
Her mind a wilderness of snares.

Who these people were, and what their names,
Not even God knows.
Other lives, million upon million,
Breeding and culling, thriving and waning;
On and on it goes.

MARCUS SEVERUS,
OF LATE MEMORY

Marcus Severus, of late memory, was so
Prodigiously endowed that
When he attended the public baths
The bathers stood and cheered.
With modest pleasure, he acknowledged this applause.

The jades of Rome, exhausted by pleasure,
Say, 'If only Severus had lived!
Then we'd have something to live for!'
But the truth is that, when he lived, no one
Remembers ever having enjoyed him.

THE BLACK FLOWER

The flower that you gave him was velvet black.
It was irresistible.
With his pious hands he touched it.
It became his body's crucible.

The flower that you gave him yielded mystery.
Its petals, double, half-concealed,
Warm and ripe,
Scented with the essence of your quintessential self,
Stole away his past
And cancelled out his history.

The flower that you gave him, black as silk,
And softer yet.
He knelt before it, hallowed it,
And paid a thousand times again
His nature's holiest debt.

THE SLAVE TELEPHUS

He's a talking diary merely,
A social secretary,
To a noble, respectable lady.
He is not your usual assassin.

If he says that he plans to kill the senate
And cut the Emperor's throat,
Don't torture him any further,
Don't even bother to kill him.
It's clear the man is mad.

It's the most common delusion of all
(Ask this of any doctor),
Thinking everyone else an impostor,
Believing oneself to be the
Only rightful emperor.

CHARITY FUNCTION

She leaned across the table, confidentially,
As the dancers whirled to the cheap band
(For this was a charity function);
And drops of rain plashed aimlessly
Outside the marquee, whilst lovers retreated
From their kissing in the lilacs
And the rhododendrons.

She took the young man's hand, toying with his fingers,
Glancing at the ham on paper plates
(For this was a charity function).
Then the rain drummed as the whole night shivered,
And nice old men in bow ties
Chatted to debutantes, and
Moths flared into the floodlights.

'Why don't you come round for a chat sometime?
I've always got some beer.' She seemed forlorn,
And his heart leaped out, for
She was middle-aged, no doubt her husband never
        touched her,
No doubt she didn't want it;
But she was strong and hale, silent and suffering, and
Someone ought to love her.
He leaned across the table, confidentially.

'I'd like that,' and it was no lie. It was
Not a charity function.
He was curious and amused,
Curious and excited, for
What could this be like?
And he was touched that he was trusted, that
It was him she asked.
It was him and not another.

LIKE IPHIGENIA

Like Iphigenia, yielding her soul for a fair voyage,
Weary she lays as she gives her body hostage
For the duration, conceding her favour a quarter hour
For a night's peace.

Over his shoulder her eyes observe the clock's hands and
The precious minutes lost to wakefulness.

He groans and heaves, and lies dead; a
Pleasure stolen and acknowledged unsatisfactory.
He wonders at such pleasure given,
So dearly bought, so hardly worth the having.

She cuts the light, curls soft flesh, tessellates
And sleeps. She has reality to cope with.
Her mind a web of obligations.
Her joys consigned to the attic trunk
With the bright clothes that once she wore
When she had time for all those things
That now are unremembered memory,
Cancelled out by all her solemn ritual practices.

Sleeping, she dreams of dusty things,
He, beside her,
Casts his memory back.

THE DOOMED BOY

He was handsome as Endymion, cast about him
The scent of virile cologne, showed brilliant teeth
When he smiled, made confident conversation,
Lived well on his father's wealth.
It was known that the women loosened their gowns and
Stroked their hair, and preened
As this beautiful man came by. They thought him
Respectful for keeping his hands to himself.
He wasn't detected down in the streets of the port,
With his ideal lips and his ideal limbs,
Whirling and dancing in basements, standing in shadows
On dim street corners, warmed briefly by transient joys,
Flitting and gliding, his hat pulled over his face
Like all the other doomed and beautiful boys.

THE FREE-FARER

When first I left my liege lord
For the ocean's wrack and the raked oar,
The straining arm and the severing wind,
I was mindful ever of my Lord's words,
That even in parting I might remain
In some sense his sworn man,
Loyal to his fief.

In many lands I wandered, witnessed
Sudden death in the hard-boned flesh of man,
Felt the keen edge of sudden joy
In the soft flesh of woman.
And always as I went my Lord's voice
Called after me in vain, for
I was far off from my Lord's land
And I no longer my Lord's man.

I will tell you this: that I will hear
All men's reasons, but my counsel is my own.
I remember this: that,
Looking back from the seaward hill,
I regretted leaving my Lord's hall
For the roofless sky and its bitter rain.
But there are oceans and noble deeds,

Merry hearths and a feast of thought
For the wise free-farer
Who leaves his lord's domain.

HER COMPLEXION

'We had,' he said, 'so much in common.
We both loved walking, loved the same songs,
Laughed at the same absurdities,
Were saddened by the same sad tales.
She made love like an angel. I've
Never known such pleasures before,
Such unexpected, novel kinds of bliss.
But I didn't keep her. I let her go. I had to.
I did it nicely. I didn't hurt her more than I should.
She'll be all right in the end.
I'm a handsome man with money. I move in certain circles.
People have expectations. One has an ideal.
A man like me is careful of reputation.
She had thin lips, a slightly poor complexion.'

POSEIDON

Cecrops: I knew him well, a reasonable king,
A maker of laws, most of them sane, some inspired,
I don't complain of him.
But his people! What can be said of them?
Those village Greeks, those peasants!
The insult they gave me – unforgiveable!
They were seeking a name for their new town
(In truth an abject collection of huts), but
I raised my trident high, I struck the ground,
And out sprang a horse, a gift, a warlike gift,
A horse on fire with youth, a horse to stir the heart,
A prancing, muscled, warlike horse.
And how those people roared!
Long live the God! Praise to the Lord of the Sea!

Athena beside me, daughter of Zeus,
My somewhat masculine niece,
Smug in virginity, conceited by reason of birth,
She raised her spear and struck the rock,
And up an olive sprang.
How they roared, those foolish men.
'Athene! The olive! Fruit of peace! The oil that makes us
        live!'

It's not as if she invented it,
That useful, ubiquitous tree,
But they named it for her, that little town,
Their newborn capital of Cecropia,
That abject collection of huts.
They chose her over me, that belligerent, termagant,
    dangerous maid,
Thinking she promised them peace
And more impressed by a tree than a beautiful, warlike
    horse.

Enraged but calm I strode away. The land shook,
As it always does when I walk, the walls crumbling,
Tiles slipping down from the roofs,
Rocks breaking off from the shore,
Cracks breaking open the earth.
Away I strode, and went and looked at the sea.

I breathed the wind, and decided: no more favours
For foolish ignorant men. And look what time has proved:
Century after century, war in that place, not peace.
Not just barbarians, also Greek against Greek.
Athena's meaningless gift!
They had greater need of my warlike horse,
Something to frighten their foes,
Those foolish, ignorant men.

TO THE SCANDAL OF POETS

A clever man, a magician in his way,
A master of sciences empiric and esoteric,
In truth, a genius,
Found an infallible method
Of reversing age,
And blocking death forever.
At the same time he found, entirely by hazard,
The exact formula to make love last.

The undertakers took it well,
Considering.
The sextons became gardeners and
Drain-layers, the ingenious lawyers found
Alternative forms of lucrative litigation.

The only ones who protested,
Who wrote eloquent letters,
Who filled the streets with banners
And threw stones at the police
Were the furious poets.
What could they possibly write of now?

THE JAILER

We saw no need to lock the cell.
I sat outside, regretting the imminent loss of
This virtuous, humorous man,
Unjustly condemned, and obsessed by the nature of truth.
I'd grown to love him, as everyone did,
This great disputer, this lover of man.
I couldn't bear to see that cup,
So well prepared, exactly the dose you need
To quell a heart, silence a tongue,
Remove a thinking man.
Simmias was there, and Phaedo and Crito.
He talked of the afterlife, the Acherusian Lake,
Tartarus, the Styx, Acheron, the Pyriphlegethon,
Such sonorous terrible dreadful names.
I shivered outside. His talk was too calm
For one meeting death before night.
He said, 'This, or something very like it
Is almost certainly true. It
Gives us hope to think so, the confidence
We need to assist us into our graves.'
I'd heard a lot of talk, him in the cell, and me outside,
Discoursing all day to his friends.
The nature of virtue, ways of the gods,
The species of lovers and loves,
The decline of passions with age.

To one such as him, such mundane, everyday things.
He went for a bath, to save the women the trouble of
Washing his corpse. He said
Farewell to his wife, his three little boys,
Instructed them all not to weep, said
'Bury me how you will, I won't be there.'
Sunset arrived. I made my little speech. I wept.
He thanked me for my care. I left
And called in the poisoner.
I didn't stay for the death, walked out in the yard.
I knew it was good, a death much
Better than most, and (as he would say) all must die
In the end. I've kept the cup.
It's there in the niche with the lares.
I pour a libation, fill it with Attican wine
And toast him, my old, entertaining, philosophical friend.
In spring I fill it with flowers. I pray for an equal end.

TIBERIUS GRACCHUS

Cornelia, how I love her! Such an elegant wife,
So dutiful, so loving, a mother of twelve,
All that pain as the penance for pleasure.
It's hard to believe it, she would never complain.
I hated her father, it was lucky he died,
Though such a great soldier he was.
She was much too young or I was too old,
But we loved each other like doves.
And then I found them, the two serpents,
Twined and writhing, there on my couch,
Harmless snakes without the venom even
To harm a rat. But what an omen it was.
I consulted diviners, soothsayers, readers of birds.
I must kill one snake. If I kill the male,
Then I will be dead. If I kill the female,
Cornelia dies. I have boiled the cauldron,
Sacrificed at the temple and thanked the lares
For all their household care.
I have made my farewells to the children, the slaves.
She has such a long time to live, I am so old.
No man has loved as I did; the water boils.
I drop the male in the pot.

THE SIN AGAINST THE
HOLY SPIRIT (I)

Jesus, Son of Mary, Prophet of Judea,
Healer, companion of the poor, a friend to all,
Having heard insulting words, all of them untrue,
Pharisaic words, ungenerous, disingenuous,
Whilst walking in the olives with his friends,
Paused for thought, sat down upon a boulder,
And sighed and shook his head.
It was then that he named the most awful of sins,
The one you never forgive, the one you cannot forget,
The one that's stored up in the soul, that later finds you
        out.
They nodded wisely, those friends, they agreed with his
        words,
But nobody knew what he meant. Peter and Thomas
Exchanged a glance, but that was all, and the Healer
Stood up and walked on. It was always hard to keep up.

HADRIAN MOURNS
ANTINOUS

No doubt they'll remember me
For the conquest of the Jews;
For abandoning Mesopotamia
(It is better to abandon what cannot be kept);
For the great walls;
For the Pantheon;
For the architects and artists;
For the Pax Romana that softened the world.

Their memories are not my own.
I remember Antinous.
Of all my lovers, ephebi and girls,
Women and men,
I remember Antinous.
Those curls that wound about the fingers,
The smooth soft flesh,
The fiercely kissing lips,
The loose, languorous, languid limbs.

They say that when I heard of his death
I wept like a woman.
But I wept like an emperor,
Ringed by assassins and slaves,
Oppressed by wealth (beyond all possible purchase),

Uncertain of the gods,
Who has lost the one sure love in life.

When the Nile surrendered his shell,
His throat over-brimmed like a jug;
Though his limbs were relaxed, as one
Exhausted after pleasure,
His eyes gazed only on Charon, the Styx,
The fifty-headed dog.
His curls lay straight,
There was sand and weed in his mouth,
And I declared him a god.

And I have made statues and temples
So that in my ceaseless travels
Through Caledonia or in Thrace,
In Gaul or Spain,
Germania,
In Alexandria of the Greeks,
In bronze and stone,
Attended by priests,
And the smoke of sacrifice
I find a place to kneel and
I find Antinous.

You may call it the grief of the omnipotent,
The indulgence of a tyrant in his solitude
(A solitude invincible and vast).
And they say that when I heard of his death

I wept like a woman.
But I wept like an emperor
Ringed by assassins and slaves,
Who has lost the one true point of light.

No doubt they'll remember me
For the conquest of the Jews,
For abandoning Mesopotamia –
It is better to abandon what cannot be kept.

Their memories are not my own.
I remember the failure to follow my own advice;
There was one I could not abandon,
Who could not be kept.

ROMANCE

'I love you,' she said, never having said it before,
And wondering what it was like; she found it
An interesting experience.

'I love you too,' he said, having said it many times
For nefarious purpose, and hoping it would
Work with her as well.

'Shall we get married?' she said, thinking of a
Bijou house, giving up her boring job,
Having kids at his expense, and becoming respectable.

'Yes, let's get married!' he said, thinking of
Regular meals, no housework, steady sex and
The novelty of adultery.

'Isn't the moon lovely?' she said, thinking of how
Like a novel it was, how very appropriate,
And impeccably romantic.

'It's shining for us!' he said suavely, dipping his
Hand inside her blouse, so that she froze before realising
It's all right, it's excusable, now that we're engaged.

'Do you really love me?' she said, nestling her head
On his tweed shoulder, as she noticed how rough
Was his hand, rotating on her breast.

'More than anything,' he said, kissing her head
On the parting, and noticing how cold
Was her breast, beneath his rotating hand.

EUTERPE

She comes uncounted times, and always in disguise.
You'll know her by the flute she carries in her hand
And by her beauty, those cascades of hair
That flow like flocks of sheep along the sides of
    mountains.
You'll know her by the music that she makes, not just
    upon her flute,
But also with her laughter in the shade among the trees.

The flowers about her head are visible or invisible,
Depending on the man who sees, depending on his eyes,
Depending on his ears,
Depending on the nature of his heart.
His eyes must be the kind that know the skies,
Perceive a hawk or crow when others see a bird.
His ears must be the kind that know the woods,
Perceive a wolf when others hear the wind.
His heart must be the kind that burns above,
Perceives the sun while others skulk in caves.

Her spirit works inside you if she loves you,
Her flame refines you, leaves you mad or glad.
She answers to Apollo, she takes her place,
A pillar in his temple. You'll find her there,
If that is what you wish, but best you find her

In the dancing of your fingers on the strings,
In all the music that you never thought you had.

THE MAN WHO TRAVELLED
THE WORLD

He travelled the world, restless as rain.
There was no continent unexplored,
Scarcely a city unworthy of days, a night, a week.
In all these places he searched for her face
In the streets, in the parks, in the lanes,
Always pausing to look, listening out
For the voice he'd never heard yet, yet
Always knew he would know.

So many lovers, so many encounters,
So many years, so many lands.

Now he sits by the window, a cat in his lap,
An ancient man far from the place of his birth.
And inside that loosening frame of bones
Beats the same heart as the heart that
Beat in the young boy who knew she was there,
And set off to travel the world.

He thinks of the children he never had,
The ordinary things foregone,
The perverseness of such an exhausting,
Such an impossible search;
A whole life squandered on dreams.

It begins to rain. He puts on his glasses,
Looks through the window, watches the girls
Step by, avoiding the puddles, protecting
Their hair with their magazines.
He fondles the ears of the cat,
This ancient man far from the place of his birth,
Still looking, still in fief to the same unsatisfied heart
As the heart that beat in the young boy
Who knew she was there and
Set off to travel the world.

ATIYA, RESPECTABLE MATRON OF ROME

Atiya, respectable matron of Rome,
(Let no one dare say otherwise)
Asleep at midnight with her ladies in the temple of Apollo,
Felt a serpent slide between her thighs and enter.

It slithered out and left, and later her belly bore
An ineradicable stain
In the unmistakeable shape of a snake.
They say that in mortification she gave up attending the
      baths, and
They say that this is proof of her mighty son's divinity.
(The cynics say she stopped because
There was no mark of the snake.)
Then Atiya, one day after feasting, dreamed
That her guts were carried to heaven,
Overspreading the world, and then
The sun rose up from in between her thighs.

As for me, what can I say? but 'Long Live the God
      Augustus'
Now that Antony has fallen on his sword.

THE REGRET OF
AN OLD MAN

I knew you before, when we were young,
You a temple maid and I an idle man.
I saw you pass in white, a circlet on your head,
And in your hands the blood-filled golden bowl.
I do confess I loved the slender grace
That still you have today.
I caught your eye and smiled. Then,
When all were glad or sick with wine
I took you to a rock and there I tried to take you.
You refused and ran.
I am glad we meet again. I doubt if you remember.
Such a long time. I was born a fool. I have always been
    sorry.
You were young and lovely. I was an idle man.

IN ALBI

It was in Albi, the time of troubadours and Raymond of
    Toulouse.
You'd taken consolamentum,
Yearning to be *parfaite*, even though we were married,
Even though I loved you, even though I hadn't finished
With my worship of your flesh, even though
Our sons had not arrived.

And so we lived, but never more we touched,
And always you refused me, and I, to keep your love,
Pretended to believe, *croyant* to your *parfaite*,
Bitter and hopeful, patient, passionate, sad.

And then the bishops took us. It was easy for me.
I'd never believed. I gave them recantation.
I gave it lightly, in truth I felt relieved.
I wore the garb they gave, I went to church,
Confessed it all, the things I'd done for love.
The kind old priest absolved me.

But you, you were *parfaite*, and in serenity you wedded to
    the flames.
You loosed your soul with joy. I stood and watched you
    burn,

And I was felled by shame. And as I stood and flinched for
     you
And wished for strength like yours to die the same as you,
You saw me through the smoke and moved your lips and
     smiled.
Those lips I'd longed for moved and mouthed those words
Whose sound was quenched by fire. I read them even so.
'*Vos am*,' you said, and I was seized by one heroic thought
And leapt towards the pyre. But even this, my single act of
     grace,
Was broken by a soldier, as I ran against his shield.

I SAW YOU IN FRANCE

I saw you in France, before the war,
At the chateau, when I was poor,
Waiting on the rich to tide me through.
I was taller then, with blacker hair,
And people thought my voice and air distinguished.
I was clothed in tails and feeling elegant, assured,
And feigning politesse.
Such a grave business, serving wine
With the white napkin and the silver tray,
And the *'Madame, vous voudriez?'*
And the *'Vous monsieur, et vous?'*
And the cries of *'Georges! Du vin!'*
Turning from the table with a laden tray,
I straightened up and saw you
In your lacy apron and your frilly cap
As you served the petits fours.
You caught my eye
And we both stood still with shock;
Some form of recognition, as I suppose,
That in forty years, in a world made new,
In altered flesh, not even in France,
At last there would be time.

I hold out my arms, drop my hands.
My eyes sting with the tears.

RUFUS GALLUS, JEW OF HEBRON

He was a Jew of Hebron
But he called himself Rufus Gallus.
He had the most wondrous resemblance
To the greatest swordsman of the day,
Undefeated in twelve consecutive games –
I mean, of course, the great Cornelius Galbus.
The same dark face, the same dark eyes,
The same stentorian voice,
Even a similar scar from eye to chin.
They say he did it himself
With the aid of a razor, Attican wine
And a mirror of polished bronze.
The mighty shoulders, the brawny arms
The thews of thighs and calves,
Were the very image of Galbus,
Even the confident stride.
Decked out in breastplate and greaves,
The magnificent plumes, the bindings of leather,
It was indeed a task to tell them apart.
Once they went to the forum together – this was their
    humour –
And invited the mob to vote for which was which.
Rufus Gallus (the Jewish impostor)
Received the same offers from women,

The same applause at the baths,
Almost the same remuneration
As the great Cornelius Galbus.
If the latter were unavailable or indisposed,
They invited the former instead,
And he stood silent, a witness to orgies and feasts
Magnificent in all his arms,
A swordsman's stern expression on his face.
The effect was the same as seeing
The real Cornelius Galbus, by which I mean
The sense of awe and honour in the guests.
No one ever thought it odd, but many remarked
How curious and generous were the gods
To have forged this Rufus Gallus, a Jew from Hebron,
Now a Roman citizen,
On the same anvil as the invincible, the great Cornelius
    Galbus.

A SAGE ADVISES A SUPPLICANT

You should instruct him how to love you:
That you do not let him crush you
With a weight and press of coils;
That he does not find himself one day,
Broken jesses trailing from his hand,
Running in your slipstream,
Calling out as you fly free.

You must instruct him, that inadvertently
He does not sting you with a viper's tooth;
That he does not cloy your tongue, overstretch his song,
And sing too sweet your praise.

You must instruct him, that he stir your memory,
That he stir your senses to precise and well-judged points,
That, in giving greatly, he does not take too much.

This is my advice. Ignore it at your peril.
Love is not a solitary study.
He will never learn to love you on his own.

FOR ONE NIGHT ONLY

When they parted they shook hands –
More final than a kiss –
In the early hours of morning
In the middle of the street.

They'd met by chance, both of them blurred by drink,
The music loud and lecherous,
The night-time heavy with the promise of debauch,
Delightful, dangerous, disreputable, delicious.

He caught her eye. There was nothing to be said.
So nothing was said. They danced, then
Hand in hand they slipped out to the beach.
The night was long. They didn't feel the cold.
The sea was blind and unconcerned,
No one came to interrupt the peace.

They lay on their clothes, sand in their hair,
Sand on their thighs and feet.
The stars ignored them. They in turn
Ignored the sea and stars. Time slowed
The tide turned. They stifled their cries,
Crammed into seven hours enough for seven years.

He was leaving. She, too, was on her way.
They parted very early in the morning, shaking hands –
More final than a kiss – in the early hours of morning
In the middle of the street.

PHILOCTETES ON HIS ISLAND

This home is not my home.
There is a word for this, and the word is 'banishment'.
These ragged, tuneless birds are not my native birds,
These famished fields are foreign fields,
This bitter land is alien land.
The water is not my own, my own was clean and cold.
The waves come in from the wrong side.
The winds have different names.
There are words for this. I am versed in all the words.
I am versed in all this solitude. My aching heart
Reminds me of my loss, my impatient friends who rowed
    away and left.
Who will cup my head in cooling hands?
Whose lips will talk away these tears?
Who will heal these stinking wounds
And gently bid me stand?
I am clothed in grief and rags and rage. My hair is wild.
But once I had seven ships.
I am the son of a king. I courted a lovely woman once,
The most prized. No one thought me unworthy,
Though another man, no better or worse than me,
Also the son of a king, finally won her hand.

MENELAOS

All those years of war, all that reeking blood,
The expense of heroes, of time and gold,
Of exhaustion, of infinite pain,
The sorrow of separation from hearth and kin,
The years away,
All to restore this truculent wife
Who pointedly turns her back,
Pretends to sleep, complains,
Weeps at table in front of the guests,
Stamps her feet and curses the day she wed.

Hector, Achilles, Patroclus!
I'd bring you all back if I could,
Haul you out of Hades,
Set the cup before you,
Express my regrets.
And her?
Honour and pride forbid, but if only I could
I'd send her back to Paris, wherever he is.
If only I knew were he was.
Dead in Hades, too, I fear.

LET HIM WITH HIS MOST REVERENT HANDS

Let him with his most reverent hands
Caress,
Let him with his most fearful thoughts
Bless
The smooth and undulating landscape
Of his lover.

To his touch she stirs, murmurs in her sleep,
Matching contours, moulding
Thigh to thigh,
Flesh to flesh, till to the last nerve they are
Indistinguishable.

The vanishing thighs, timid as a faun,
And the heat of sleep
Warm and wake his sense,
But it's too late now for drowsy embarkations.
This lock upon her temple, then,
Let him kiss for recompense.

May the day not come,
May the dawn wither, severed at the root;
May it leave them still,
She sleeping, he awake,

She dreaming of love, her love enfolding her,
Dreaming that she loves him.

IT ENDED

It ended. He didn't know why.
It happens. The leaves fall away.
Someone makes a mistake.
Someone's expelled.
Someone revises their dream.

So now he quests for the same eyes
In another face that must also be the same.
He seeks out lips that remind him.
He wakes at night, having dreamed
That nothing was wrong.
He slides out of bed, leans on the sill,
Blames the moon for subverting his sleep,
Closes his eyes, imagines her there,
Out on the lawn, out in the cold,
Back in the bed, not lost at all,
If only sleep would return.

THE OLD ONES

We cut down the groves
And made fires and beams for our houses.
Of the golden sickles
We made bracelets and rings
For the boxes of Christian ladies.
We took the stones, and some we broke
For our walls;
Others we built into churches.
We lost the means of reading runes,
There was no more rutting on feast days
In token or in true.

There is no memory of any of it now.
We put it behind us, convinced by new stories,
Exotic languages,
Yet more extravagant mysteries.
There was incense, candles and bells,
And the irresistible offer of hope.

But the old ones have by no means gone.
It is still this island that they love.
It is we who are remembered
At those times in spring or autumn,
Midsummer or winter,
When their ever-youthful souls stand wistful,

Holding hands
In the shade of long-demolished groves.
Sometimes, indeed, a vigorous shadow
Vaults a stream or
Leaps from the crown of hills.

THE SIN AGAINST THE
HOLY SPIRIT (2)

I met a traveller from an antique land, who said
'I know what it is. I know what the Healer meant:
That terrible sin, the one you never forgive,
The one you cannot forget, the one that's stored in the
    soul
And will later find you out. It all came clear in a dream.
I remember the Healer well, it was me he loved the best.
I'm certain he sent this dream. At last I know what it is!
But no, I cannot divulge it. I am not allowed to explain.
You must find it out for yourself: travel through life,
Be a victim of follies and crimes, take forks in the road,
Wait for the revelation, or deduce it from struggle and
    pain.'

THE SEPARATION

She is lovely like a faun.
He sees her in the long grass,
In the dark window of her empty room,
In the narrow bed
(Vacant even when shared).
He detects her in the young girls' faces
He searches in the street, and
He hears her when another woman laughs.
He catches her fetch,
Seated by the fire
In the favourite chair.
He sees her when a woman is wearing green.
He expects her when doors and windows are windblown
    wide,
But only the whirling leaves
And only the world are there.

He was hardly lovely
(Even when greatly loved) and
Yet in his greedy hands
A beautiful hunger was born.
She travels away and never arrives.
He is there in his absence in
All those sunshot lands.
She hears him in lucid, falsely predictive dreams,

She senses his weight at dawn,
Feverish still when the harbour wakes,
The ships' horns boom
And the first seagull screams.

PHILETAS THE PASTORALIST AND GRAMMARIAN

So thin I grew, poor hermit that I was,
So little compensated for my learning and my verse,
That friends had leaden sandals made,
To keep me earthbound when the tempests blew.

Scanter still am I, who now in Kos lies dead,
The wind of death being undeterred by lead.

A DEATH FOREKNOWN

He knew about her lies, her subterfuge,
Her many deceptions, her blatant schemes,
Evasions, her tricks and machinations,
The strange indifference to another human heart.
He didn't care; her body was so sweet,
Her tiny kisses light and soft,
The electric touch, cool caresses,
The shivers up his spine.
He thought of little else, and wanted nothing else,
That flesh was all the universe to him.
And this is why, the evening that she told him of
Her other love for whom she had to leave,
He calmly went and fetched the things,
Laid them out before him, checked that all was there,
The lethal things he'd hidden months before,
Prepared against this bitter day
He always knew would come.

YOUR BRIGHTON DRESS

I remember that dress: it was Brighton, a summer's day,
Out in the street,
Hung on a rack almost above our heads.
Your eyes lit up. It was just your kind of dress.
Heavy fabric, soft and brown, exactly
The shade you liked, the colour of
Melancholy, the colour of 1979;
The year for people like us,
A couple without a map,
A country with nowhere to go,
That had lost the art of laughing,
Didn't have muscle to breathe.

In all the world I'd twelve pounds left,
But I bought the dress, for your body's sake,
For the sake of your eyes' delight. It was a bridge,
A perfect bridge for gentle sweet desires.
You loved me for the gifting of the dress. I loved you
For your gratitude, your disbelieving face,
Your little leaps of happiness.

I have often remembered
How off you went, so many months, off in search of
    yourself.
Then back you came, let yourself in with your own key.

It was late at night, it was almost dawn, you teased me
    awake with a kiss.

Such slices of time have fallen away. I've scarcely seen you
For longer than we'd been alive.
It was back in a former life, but I like to remember,
False though this may be,
That when I woke up and you were there,
You were bringing me Mexican presents,
Wearing a silver necklace,
Wearing your Brighton dress.

TWENTY YEARS ON

Twenty years on I went out and looked at the house
The house where I lay with her, loved
With all my eager heart, endured
The torture of all that unappeasable lust.
How strong my body was, what stinging flame
Burned bright in my bones, how then
My hands gripped hard on life.

How strange that these drab bricks,
These peeling sills, these stained walls,
Housed within them such
Tornados of desire, that even now I
Think this ordinary place is
Drenched in what still lingers,
What remains, though nothing at all
Remains.

ONE WHO DIED UNEXPECTEDLY OF NATURAL CAUSES

He was not in love with this life.
He planned to die a Roman's death.
His sword was honed, his friends informed,
The judgement made, yet no time set.
His eyes were ready for the final sleep,
His lungs were practised for the long last breath.
But not quite yet.

WHAT LOVE DOES

This is what love does. This is what you say:
'Behold I love you in all languages, in all hearts and in all
    stars.
I am spread skyward to mate with the moon, swarm with
    the sea,
Convulse with the fire of the sun.
Behold, I walk unharmed in the flames of joy
And even the clang of silence stays unheard.
Behold, I talk with God to God's face
And fly with angels in a further sky.'
Enjoy it as long as you can. You'll remember it fondly,
This flying with angels, this chatting with God on equal
    terms.

ANOTHER HOUSE

You said, 'I will go to another house, to another place.
This one isn't mine. I've been buried in its walls.
I can't remain here. I see nothing that I chose,
Nothing that's refreshing to my eyes,
No one that I haven't been with every day for years.
How much the time went by, escaped my grasp.
How much was ruined, left to die, how much of life
I wasted in this wilderness, this house that wasn't mine.'

You'll find no other house, no other place.
These walls will follow you. It will always be the same,
And you'll grow old with the same longing, the same
        solitude,
Grow grey in the same mismanagement,
Forever in the self-same walls, the walls you packed into
        your bags.
Do not go hoping for a better road, a lusher meadow,
You could not leave and leave yourself behind.
As you have ruined your life, here within these walls,
You have ruined it everywhere, anywhere,
Wherever you are in the world, in another place,
Another house that also isn't yours.

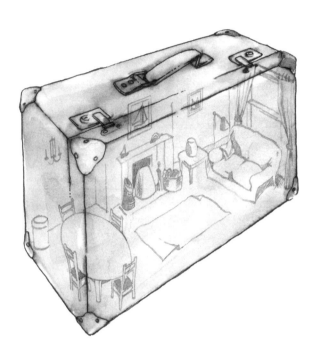

WILD WHITE LIGHT

Don't touch the god, even if he loves you.
You would fall sick of pleasure,
Overflow, become consumed and die.
You would incandesce
With a wild white light.

Don't touch the god, even if he loves you –
Just look upon your treasure,
The precious coin you gloat above.
Stand back, amazed,
Breathing in his wild white light.

Don't touch the god, even if he loves you –
Don't shape and measure,
Lay on hands, tease out delight,
Approach too close,
Burst to atoms in the wild white light.

Everyone touches the god in the end.
It's irresistible, the temptation, but
You might be saved.
Don't touch the god, even if he loves you.

LEONIDAS THE TARENTINE ADDRESSES THE TWO MICE

Dear mice, respect my trade.
I am a poet. Poets need to eat.
I have one dirty lump of salt, a little old,
And barley cake is all I have for meat.

Dear mice, go bite on someone else's cakes.
A lawyer or a usurer, innocent of verse,
Unburdened by philosophy,
Who dines on hogs and quails,
Whose stomach never aches.

THEIR MUTUAL VOWS

He promised to love her forever,
If she would be always young,
If she would be always new,
Always exquisite;
If she could charm his sense
With infinite variety;
If she could make him smile
Unceasingly for sixty years.
And she, she promised in turn
To love him forever,
With most of her heart,
For the time being,
For much of the time.

A PRAYER

God preserve us from the unclean chastity of priests,
For I would be whole and joyful,
Knowing as I do that dust awaits my flesh,
Knowing as I do that damp awaits my bones,
And all the chastity a priest could ask,
Imposed forever. Clay and wood and
Yew tree shade and yew tree root and stones. So
God reward us with the honest joy of beasts, and
God preserve us from the unclean chastity of priests.

AT THE SORBONNE

He walked these streets the first time
(He was young and handsome then)
With a woman he betrayed,
And the streets remind him of her golden hair,
Her easy ways, the black stone set in the silver ring.

He bought Montaigne, white sausage.
It was Christmas. They'd bought a duck
And cooked it badly.
These were the times when
Intellectuals gathered in cafés,
Avid for seduction,
Talked of revolution,
Ranged in the Latin Quarter, smoked for the sake of style.
You might perhaps run into Roland, Jean-Paul and Simone.
Georges was writing songs.
It was after Albert crashed and died.

There was no hot water, this was Paris;
The sewage breathed from the grates;
The women went out with their poodles.
The coffee was perfect, the cafés warm:
The Café Rodin
The Café Louvre
The Café Jeu de Paumes.

They kissed in the dark, oblivious;
They kissed in the light, in public, mischievous.
They made love and made love and made love;
Youth eternal, the hunger immense,
The years ahead so long,
Faith and hope unquenched.

When they came home the pipes were iced;
The cats brought gifts of rabbits,
Voles and mice and woodcock.
They boiled a kettle, melted the ice,
Lit the fire, went out and ate,
Came back to shivering sheets.

Later, betrayal. It all came later;
Her penitential tears, her hair falling about her eyes,
Her features crooked with remorse, her musician's hands
Trembling on his shoulders.
He was correct and stiff, but
Found it easy to forgive.
He was grateful, after a fashion;
It gave him his excuse.

When he considers the many, the substitutes
Who left, reciting their lists of lovers;
When he walks these streets,
Scarcely believing the slippage,
He then remembers the gold-haired girl,
With her easy ways, her musician's hands,
Her penitential tears, her kisses.

TWO THOUSAND NIGHTS

You said, 'Two thousand nights I've lain beside that form.
They were rare as unicorns, the kisses, the embraces;
Her back turned, my roving hands unlicensed,
Her hand restraining mine.
In another room, my confusion, my solitary tears.
I travelled as far as heaven, foresaw such a beautiful life.
I stood at the gate, reached out my hand for the latch,
The latch that rusted and seized.'
So, recollecting how she span away, attached herself
        elsewhere,
Greater moon to lesser sun, do not gloss over, from
        yourself do not conceal
The looted time, the several clever kinds of theft.
If back she spins, bringing her beauty, should her lovely
        voice
(Ever gentle, soft and low) sound once again in your silent
        rooms,
Should you long for her breasts, her belly's curve, her
        illegible eyes,
The bright scent of her hair,
Beware the temptation. Ponder the cancelled dreams.
Steady your heart. Beware the hope that lures, then bites.
Do not say, 'The Gods condemned me to love her. What
        choice do I have?'

Only the Gods can know what they did. My friend, beware temptation,
Remember the sleepless darkness, the looted time;
Consider the debt to pleasure; remember the two thousand nights.

I CAUSED THIS TOMB
TO BE MADE

I caused this tomb to be made against the day of my death,
In the Lycian style,
With forethought for my sons, and the great expense.
For, great though I may be, like any other sage,
Any other king, dreamer, prophet, poet,
Like any peasant, any dog, I trudge or dance the same
    wide road.

I caused this tomb to be made in the form of a ship
    upturned,
Slab-sided, vast, mounted on blocks, inscribed with noble
Words, lists of honours gained.

Reflect that once it breathed, the dust within,
Once they walked, the bones.

I set this tomb in the street, at the widest point,
Planted figs for fruit and shade.
I caused a bench to be made in stone,
And carved a trough for rain.
If any require it, let water be brought.
If any should have the skill,
Then let them speak these words
To those that cannot read.

Earthquake and wave undo all things,
Even this tomb may fail and fall.

In the shade of this fig, when time permits,
When office allows,
I will sit in the swelter of noon
By my own tomb, and think of what it may mean to
Be sealed and silent within these walls
As all my wealth disperses, all my fame falls off,
And the fig tree grows.

LEONIDAS OF ALEXANDRIA

By Nero, Agrippina, and Poppea
I set much store, and they set store by me.
My verses and my epigrams amused –
They were flattered, touched and pleased.
I glowed in the light of the great.
How many hours with a flask of wine
By the light of a lamp I gave to my clever isopsepha!
How worthless they seem to me now.

The poets and painters loved me,
Honoured by satire, the private digs in the ribs.
I could write you an ode to your nose –
It would cost you the price of a meal.
I could write you a comic tale
Of an old man cursed in a young wife.

If the god permits, after my death,
I will write in Hades the rolling,
Wonderful, grandiloquent, sensitive,
Lyrical, moving verse, that, for all my success,
I never could write in life.

IN DENTON CHURCHYARD

Death has dark wings, composed of shadow,
Articulated, huge;
So huge that sometimes things are touched by accident
And destiny denied.
Death will make an appointment,
Sets up his rendezvous.
Death means no harm, is not malicious,
But he has his own chains,
The rails he has to roll on, the role he has to play.
He's sorry, sir, but he's only doing his job.
He can't come back at a more convenient time.
And Death regrets the loss of beauty, loss of talent,
End of promise, hearts impaled
By shards and darts, on blades and spikes of grief.
Death deplores himself in truth;
In place of dust, he longs to taste life's sugar on his tongue.
Death is denied the rest he forces on the rest; therefore
He flies forever on dark wings composed of shadow
Articulated, huge.

Love is weaker than Death;
Love has crystal wings.

STONE HOTEL

The stone hotel in that Yorkshire town –
The site of our first tryst,
Not far from the park and the wood
And the river that runs by the graves –
I would think you remember it well.

I'd booked two rooms in case it was wrong,
In case your mind was changed,
But you came to mine, and I was seized
By your slender bones, your long gold hair
That curtained your cheeks, that fell to your waist,
That you liked to use as a whip,
The most exquisite, painless lash in the world.

You told me tales of becoming bewitched,
Of your mad mother, your luckless father,
Your home in the wilds,
The shotgun under the bed.

It was the first tryst, the first of too few nights,
And we were foiled by distance, by prior commitment,
Events that spun out of control.

I am writing to tell you that I took the wrong path –
Always did and always will –

And I've just been back, and they've boarded it up,
Our stone hotel that's near to the river
That runs by the wood and the park and the graves.
They're boarding it up and making flats,
Without regard or respect for the room or the bed
Where once we lay and loved and talked
All night on our first night,
So long ago on our first tryst
When we were careless and bold.

NOSSIS OF LOCRIS

I am Nossis of Locris, the bronze of my heart annealed by
    flame.
Go tell them in Kos, in Chios, in Antioch, in Cyprus, and
Above all in Lesbos, that
All I ever did was Aphrodite's will.
I burned like Sappho, earned an equal fame.
I burned and loved and wrote as well as she.

All my work is lost.
Remember me.

WHEN THE TIME COMES

When the time comes, it is better that death be welcome,
As an old friend who embraces and forgives.
Sieze advantage of what little time is left,
And if imagination serves, if strength endures, if memory
    lives,
Ponder on those vanished loves, those jesting faces.
Take once more their hands and press them to your cheek,
Think of you and them as young again, as running in the
    fields,
As drinking wine and laughing.
And if you wish, let there be Spanish music, Greek seas
And French sun, the hills of Ireland if you loved them,
Some other place if that should please, some other music
More suited to your taste.
Consider, if you can, that
Soon you'll shed this weariness, this pain,
The heaped-upon indignities, and afterwards – who
    knows? –
Perhaps you'll walk with angels, should angels be,
By fresher meadows, unfamiliar streams.
You may find that those who did not love you do so now,
That those who loved you did so more than you believed.
You may go on to better lives and other worlds.
You may meet God, directly or disguised.

You may, on the other hand – who knows? – just wander
    off
To sleep that seamless, darkest, dreamless, unimaginable
    sleep.
Do not be bitter, no world lasts forever.
You who travelled like Odysseus,
This is Ithaca, this your destination,
This your last adventure. Here is my hand,
The living to the dying;
Yours will grow cold in mine, when the time comes.